ABSTRACT
DESIGNS COLORING BOOK

BRIAN JOHNSON

DOVER PUBLICATIONS, INC.
MINEOLA, NEW YORK

This assortment of interesting abstract designs was rendered with the experienced colorist in mind. Select your media, and use the detailed images of interlocking and overlapping shapes, spirals, swirls, and more, to experiment with color usage and technique. Plus, the perforated, unbacked pages make displaying your work easy!

Bibliographical Note

Abstract Designs Coloring Book is a new work, first published by
Dover Publications, Inc., in 2014.

International Standard Book Number

ISBN-13: 978-0-486-77956-0
ISBN-10: 0-486-77956-4

Manufactured in the United States by LSC Communications
77956405   2019
www.doverpublications.com